Summary & Analysis: For the Love

Fighting for Grace in a World of Impossible Standards

By Jen Hatmaker

Authored by Instaread

Instaread on For the Love

Please Note

This is a summary and analysis.

Copyright © 2015 by Instaread. All rights reserved worldwide. No part of this publication may be reproduced or transmitted in any form without the prior written consent of the publisher.

Limit of Liability/Disclaimer of Warranty: The publisher and author make no representations or warranties with respect to the accuracy or completeness of these contents and disclaim all warranties such as warranties of fitness for a particular purpose. The author or publisher is not liable for any damages whatsoever. The fact that an individual or organization is referred to in this document as a citation or source of information does not imply that the author or publisher endorses the information that the individual or organization provided. This concise summary is unofficial and is not authorized, approved, licensed, or endorsed by the original book's author or publisher.

Table of Contents

OVERVIEW 4
IMPORTANT PEOPLE 6
KEY TAKEAWAYS 7
ANALYSIS 9
Key Takeaway 1 9
Key Takeaway 2 11
Key Takeaway 3 13
Key Takeaway 4 15
Key Takeaway 5 17
Key Takeaway 6 19
Key Takeaway 7 21
Key Takeaway 8 23
Key Takeaway 9 25
Author's Style 28
Author's Perspective 29
References 30

OVERVIEW

For the Love: Fighting for Grace in a World of Impossible Standards by Jen Hatmaker is a self-help book about women's pursuit of perfection.

In the modern world, most women have the opportunity to do and be whatever they set their minds to. If a woman wants to be a chief executive officer (CEO), she can be a CEO. If a woman wants to be a stay-at-home mom, she can be a stay-at-home mom. However, this land of opportunity has also given rise to the idea that women can have it all, be it all, and be successful in every aspect of their lives, all by themselves. Unfortunately, this is not possible, but that has not stopped women from running themselves ragged in the pursuit of perfection. In order to live a fulfilled and happy life, women need to come to terms with the fact that society's standards are impossible to meet, and then figure out what they truly want to do, while finding ways to delegate the rest.

Furthermore, as women find grace for themselves, they need to extend this same grace to others. Indeed, no one is perfect, everyone has unique traits that may conflict with those around them, and expecting anyone to maintain the standards of society is unreasonable. Finally, as women learn to live in grace, they must work at forming true and lasting relationships that are based on love and acceptance, not competition. This will lead to a happy, and fulfilled, life.

IMPORTANT PEOPLE

Jen Hatmaker: Married with five children, Hatmaker decided she wanted more from life and chose to pursue her passion for writing. This lead to a number of books, including the bestsellers, *7: An Experimental Mutiny Against Excess*, and *For the Love:Fighting for Grace in a World of Impossible Standards*.

KEY TAKEAWAYS

1. The idea that women can do it all, perfect it all, and have it all is a farce that destroys happiness. Women need to choose to do the things they love and excel at, delegate the rest, and let go of the guilt that comes from thinking they have to be perfect in every area of their lives.

2. When women compare themselves to others it only leads to resentment and pain. Women need to learn to be happy with who they are, and to be happy for others.

3. God's calling for a woman's life is to love, live the life that she has been given, and pursue her own gifts and talents.

4. Women need to ignore the messages that say they are not good enough, thin enough, or pretty enough. The media's portrayal of women is not real, and trying to attain that standard is a waste of time and effort.

5. Women need to stop acting like everything is perfect, and be honest with themselves and others.

6. Women need to stop over-criticizing themselves when it comes to parenting.

7. A healthy marriage takes work.

8. Having friends and being a friend to others is vitally important. However, women also need to learn to let go of people who thrive on drama and are toxic.

9. While the church is the body of Christ, people need to recognize that it is made up of humans who are capable of failing and hurting others.

ANALYSIS

Key Takeaway 1

The idea that women can do it all, perfect it all, and have it all is a farce and destroys happiness. Women need to choose to do the things they love and excel at, delegate the rest, and let go of the guilt that comes from thinking they have to be perfect in every area of their lives.

Analysis

In the modern world, women often feel the need to have it all, do it all, and be perfect in every area of their lives. Some women feel the need to have stellar careers, be a nurturing mother who feeds her kids organic and nutritious, gourmet meals three times a day, be part of the parent teacher association (PTA), lead the booster club, volunteer at the local food pantry, and maintain a perfect physique, to boot. This pursuit of perfection in every area of a woman's life is not only destructive as it is impossible to attain, but when a women inevitably fails, she feels guilty, and that destroys happiness.

In fact, women who try to have it all are miserable. They have become so caught up in the pursuit of perfection that they run themselves ragged and miss out on what matters most in life. As such, women need to learn to focus on what is most important to them, delegate that which they do not want to do or are not good at, and be graceful with themselves. This is to say, if a woman wants to be a stay-at-home, nurturing mother, she needs to accept that a career as a CEO may not be possible. Conversely, if a woman wants to be a CEO of a Fortune 500 company, she needs to recognize, and be okay with, the fact that she may not have time for every childhood activity. Simply put, women need to realize and accept that they cannot possibly do it all by themselves [1].

Key Takeaway 2

A young woman may spend a great deal of time allowing others to define who she is. But with maturity comes the understanding that everyone is uniquely different and comparisons are a waste of time.

Analysis

Reaching the age of forty is a difficult milestone for many women. They begin to resemble the older women in their lives they once swore they would never turn into. They lose track of societal trends. They yell at younger people for doing the same things they themselves once did. They become what they always swore they would not: middle aged. However, with age and maturity also comes resiliency. Once a woman hits a certain age, she begins to realize that comparing herself to others is simply a waste of time. It does not matter what others think because once a woman reaches this age, she finally knows who she is, what she wants, and what matters most to her. And when a woman understands these things, she no longer needs to compare herself to others.

The compulsive need for people to compare themselves to others often stems from insecurity. When a person does not feel confident in who they are, as can come from not really understanding who they are, they can look to others for guidance. This is evident in high school students who often dress, talk, and act like their friends because they want to fit in. High school students have not yet figured out who they are and who they want to be as they age. For this reason, they do what everyone else is doing. This can sometimes be dangerous as others might judge them for who they choose to emulate or for not emulating that person perfectly.

With maturity comes insight into self. As most women mature, they begin to understand and accept their own values and morals, to embrace their own choices and actions, and to become their own person. By the age of forty, a majority of women no longer care what others might think. And this leads to grace in a woman's life as it allows them more time for the things that really matter, such as family.

Key Takeaway 3

God's calling for a woman's life is to love, live the life that she has been given, and pursue her own gifts and talents.

Analysis

Christian women often have the belief that they need to discover God's calling for their life, and if they do not discover this calling they will not complete the purpose that God has for them. Unfortunately, this search for a calling sometimes results in women pressing pause on their lives while they await God's instruction.

However, scripture does not define a calling besides saying to live a worthy life. Consequently, constantly searching for God's specific purpose for a person's life is folly. A woman's calling is to love others, live her life to the best of her ability, and pursue the gifts and talents God gave her.

In this way, every woman's calling is different because every woman's life and talents are different. For example, some women are naturally creative and will excel at helping out with plays at school, or in the local community theater. Other women are naturally nurturing and will excel at lending an ear where it is needed, or going into counseling. Still others are naturally good at leading, and can take control of projects and people to lead them to success.

The idea is simply that women do not need to constantly be on the lookout for some elusive calling. Living the life that has been given, living it to the best of a person's ability, and living in the now results in living a worthy life, which is a woman's calling [3].

Key Takeaway 4

Women need to ignore the messages that say they are not good enough, thin enough, or pretty enough. The media's portrayal of women is not real, and trying to attain that standard is a waste of time and effort.

Analysis

The media portrays women in ads as perfect, beautiful, fun, and youthful, and simultaneously sends the message that the women watching the ad or program are not these things because they do not have product being sold, or are not like model who appears in the ad. This is a marketing ploy and must be recognized as such. The women in the ads, or on TV, are not a real representation of women. Models and actors have been airbrushed, have a team of stylists, health coaches, and makeup artists to make them appear as they do. As such, trying to attain the standard that they represent is a waste of time and effort.

In fact, the media often depicts women who are well below a healthy body weight, and labels these models and actors as ideal. Studies have shown that the media is rife with images that portray the ideal woman as blonde, tall, thin, white, and curvy in the right places. This is an unrealistic standard of beauty, but the bombardment of these images makes it seem like this standard is attainable for the average women. This is untrue, and this ideal sends the unspoken message that if a woman wants to be beautiful, she must find a way to attain the impossible standard. In other words, do what it takes, even if it is unhealthy.

More importantly, when a woman allows herself to be constantly exposed to the media's ideal it is dangerous. Studies have conclusively shown that women are negatively affected by the perpetual exposure to models that satisfy the media's unrealistic ideal for beauty. Consequently, women need to be cognizant of what they are being exposed to, and recognize and reject the media's portrayal of women. By doing so, women can learn to appreciate their own beauty and be happy with who they are [4].

Key Takeaway 5

Women need to stop acting like everything is perfect and be honest with themselves and others.

Analysis

Sometimes women do not tell the truth about who they are or what they are feeling because they are afraid of being judged or abandoned. However, when a woman learns to tell the truth about herself, her struggles, and her fears, she experiences freedom and healing.

When women tell the truth about themselves, it frees others to do the same. If a woman is always acting like everything is perfect, her friends may feel like they cannot voice their own struggles. But when women learn to be open and honest, it creates an environment where others can also be open and honest.

For example, if a women portrays to her friends that her family is perfect, her house is perfect, her job is perfect, and she is perfect, all while her marriage is on the rocks, the bank is about to repossess her house, her kids are suffering, and she feels like life is not worth living, she not only misses out on the help she could receive from her friends, but she also misses out on connection with friends who may be suffering similar situations. Additionally, her similarly suffering friends may feel like they cannot talk to their perfect friend for fear of being judged, even though the perfect friend is an emotional wreck behind closed doors. But if this woman chooses to lose the persona of perfection, she not only gains emotional support, she also connects on a deeper level with her friends. This brings about healing, and it frees the women from acting like everything is perfect.

More importantly, women are emotional beings, and when they hide their true feelings, they lose touch with who they really are. However, when women are honest with themselves and others, they learn more about who they truly are. This leads to greater self-love, and acceptance [5].

Key Takeaway 6

Women need to stop over-criticizing themselves when it comes to parenting.

Analysis

Many good mothers worry that they are not doing a decent job raising their children, and observing other perfect families in public can often exacerbate this concern. However, women need to realize that they are not seeing the full picture. Other families also face their fair share of problems, even if outsiders do not observe it. Consequently, women need to stop comparing their families and children to other families and children, stop over-criticizing themselves, and recognize that they are probably doing a better job than they think.

There are no perfect families. What a woman sees when she is over at another mom's house or out doing errands is only a snippet of that other woman's time. For example, a woman may see another woman's children listening and behaving perfectly at the grocery store and assume that woman's children are angels. However, that woman with the angel children may go home, walk in the door, and her children start fighting with one another and running wild around the house. Of course, the woman who observed the angel children at the grocery store sees none of this. She only sees a brief glimpse and assumes because her own children are climbing all over the shopping cart that she is somehow failing at parenting.

No one is born knowing how to parent. It is a skill that is learned in the process of parenting, so it is natural for a woman to question herself. However, it is important to understand that every family has its own issues that it has to deal with, and these issues are not always on display. Consequently, women need to recognize that they need to have grace with themselves, and not be so hard on themselves. Other women also struggle with parenting [6].

Key Takeaway 7
A healthy marriage takes work.

Analysis

Marriage is the joining of two people who love each other, but who likely have different opinions and ways of viewing the world. As such, sustaining a happy marriage takes work. It also takes keeping in mind the fact that each person will have different strengths and weakness, will like different things, and will fight in different ways. As such, things that help keep a marriage strong are finding good friends, being nice to one another even when irritated, going to church and staying one the same level spiritually, having fun together, and having lots of sex.

The above is to say that women need to recognize that the men they married do not need to be fixed to better meet their standards. Similarly, women do not need to be fixed to better meet the standards of their men. This is not to say people should not grow and adjust to better accommodate their spouse in certain ways. It is to say that both people need to recognize that there will always be differences between two individuals because that is the way God made them. Furthermore, these differences are not broken pieces in need of repair. By accepting this, women will experience more harmony in their marriage.

In fact, many experts agree that learning to choose battles carefully is vitally important to maintaining a healthy marriage. No matter how much people love each other, they will inevitably differ on some things. Consequently, if a woman wants her marriage to work, she has to accept this and not squabble over every little difference because her husband is not exactly the same as she [7].

Additionally, it is important to retain the spark that led to love in the first place. This means couples need to purposefully have fun together and do things that build happy memories and deeper connections. For example, going on dates, finding couples that enjoy the same things, and going to church together help keep couples in line with each other. This leads to deeper love and commitment.

Key Takeaway 8

Having friends and being a friend to others is vitally important. However, women also need to learn to let go of people who thrive on drama and are toxic.

Analysis

Thanks to social media, in-person relationships are becoming optional. However, this type of relationship is not a substitute for getting together with friends and connecting in person. In fact, connecting face-to-face with friends is essential for a woman. But, while friendships should be an important part of a woman's life, learning to let go of toxic friends is also important.

There are people who thrive on drama and will go out of their way to create drama even if drama does not exist. Likewise, there are people who make themselves feel better by constantly putting others down. This is not a healthy person and being around that person will have a negative impact on a woman's life.

If a woman's friend is constantly trying to sow discord amongst friends by gossiping about other women behind their backs, and then spreading what is said, this will likely result in fights. These fights are not only destructive to the friendship, but they also cause unnecessary stress and anger amongst friends. In this way, the gossiping friend is a drama instigator and it would be better to end the friendship.

Likewise, if a woman's friend is constantly telling her how fat, horrible, and worthless she is, this constant message will likely have an impact on a woman's self-esteem. The friendship is toxic and it would be better to end the friendship [8].

Key Takeaway 9

While the church is the body of Christ, women need to recognize that it is made up of humans who are capable of failing and hurting others.

Analysis

The early church started out as a group of believers who got together for fellowship, communion, and teaching. Unfortunately, somewhere along the line, some churches became productions where pastors are infallible entertainers, the size of the congregations and the special programs are a bragging point, and the congregation has expectations that must be met. This is not the purpose of the church.

Indeed, this type of church projects the image that it is perfect, its pastor is perfect, and its members are perfect that not only leads to unrealistic expectations, it also leaves people hurting with nowhere to turn. Specifically, when members of a congregation expect the church and its other members to be perfect, they do not extend grace to people who are hurting within the church and in the community.

If women expect their pastor to be perfect, that pastor may feel forced to hide his own struggles or face the possibility of letting down his congregation. Consequently, his issues cannot be expressed and dealt with because of the unrealistic expectations of the congregation. Further, because these struggles and issues are never brought to light, they will likely continue to fester and grow. Additionally, if women expect other women of the congregation to be perfect, women who are struggling with their own issues may feel like they have to hide their sin and maintain the façade of a perfect Christian. This also results in that woman's sin festering.

Conversely, a woman may be struggling with sin and bring it to the other members for prayer, help, and healing only to receive condemnation and ostracization simply for failing to live up to the perfect Christian expectations of the congregation. This is not how Christ behaved, and it is not how the church is supposed to treat its members [9].

Women need to stop expecting their churches, pastors, and fellow church members to be perfect and see the church for what it is, a gathering of people with problems, led by someone who is human and also has problems, and who together are walking faith's path while providing love and help to each other and their community.

Author's Style

Jen Hatmaker is a hilarious writer; the kind who literally makes the reader laugh out loud at her stories. But, while her stories are funny, most of them also carry an important message. For example, Hatmaker gives thanks to Spanx and its unnatural body-molding ability, as well as its ability to take her breath away. This is how Hatmaker points out that she literally has a hard time breathing when she wears shapewear, but suffers through because society requires that her body be a certain shape, even after bearing children. It is this combination of humor and underlying message that creates a pleasurable reading experience.

Further, Hatmaker uses stories from her own experiences to draw the reader in and help the reader relate to the points in the story. In addition, Hatmaker is not afraid to display her own worries, fears, and insecurities as well as what she struggles with, which lends her an air of credibility. Plus, her writing is clear, to the point, and engaging.

Author's Perspective

For the Love is funny and helpful because of Jen Hatmaker's unique perspectives. The daughter of a former pastor, married to a current pastor, a wife, a mother, and a working speaker and writer, Hatmaker has faced, and is keenly aware, of the pressures placed on women both by the church and society. In fact, Hatmaker points out that when she speaks at conferences, many women ask her how she does it all. Her response is that she has help. Indeed, it is questions like these that caused Hatmaker to realize that there are many women struggling to have it all, only to fail and then face guilt. Consequently, Hatmaker wrote *For the Love* to help bring to light this struggle and point out that women can have it all, but they cannot do it by themselves, and that is okay.

~~~~~~ END OF INSTAREAD~~~~~~~

References

1. Russell, Nicole. "Women Can't Have It All, But They Can Have What Matters." *The Federalist*. March 13, 2015, accessed September 9, 2015. http://thefederalist.com/2015/03/13/women-cant-have-it-all-but-they-can-have-what-matters/
2. Brown, Sienna. "Reclaiming Sisterhood: Why Women Shouldn't See Each Other As Competitors, But As Allies." *Elite Daily Reclaiming Sisterhood Why Women Shouldn't See Each Other As Competitors But As Allies Comments*. March 4, 2014, accessed September 9, 2015. http://elitedaily.com/women/reclaiming-sisterhood-why-women-shouldnt-see-each-other-as-competitors-but-as-allies/
3. Perkins, Paul. "Stop Waiting for Your Calling and Start Living." *The Huffington Post*. August 17, 2014, accessed September 9, 2015. http://www.huffingtonpost.com/paul-perkins/stop-waiting-for-your-cal_b_5654486.html

4. Serdar, Kasey. "Female Body Image and the Mass Media: Perspectives on How Women Internalize the Ideal Beauty Standard." *The Myriad: Westminster's Interactive Academic Journal*. Westminster College, accessed September 9, 2015. http://www.westminstercollege.edu/myriad/index.cfm?parent=...&detail=4475&content=4795

5. Elizabeth, Tamara. "Understanding the Self-Confident Authentic Woman." *Divine Caroline*, accessed September 9, 2015. http://www.divinecaroline.com/self/self-discovery/understanding-self-confident-authentic-woman

6. "Why Become One?" *Nobody's Perfect*, accessed September 9, 2015. http://www.nobodysperfect.ca/innerpage.aspx?x=4rjcjqA%2FdaEl9kP2NPgy1%2FP2tmOGfRR9FcQxjIwDnxP2ljqnMdkXsDn%2BO3N9p4OS

7. Grohol, John. "5 Secrets to a Successful Long-Term Relationship or Marriage." *Psych Central*. January 13, 2013, accessed September 10, 2015. http://psychcentral.com/lib/5-secrets-to-a-successful-long-term-relationship-or-marriage/?all=1

8. Feature, Heather. "Toxic Friendships: Do You Have One? - WebMD." *WebMD*, accessed September 10, 2015. http://www.webmd.com/women/features/toxic-friends-less-friend-more-foe

9. Wagner, Kimberly. "When the Church Hurts You." *True Woman*. April 30, 2015, accessed September 10, 2015. http://www.truewoman.com/?id=3148

Made in the USA
Lexington, KY
11 February 2016